# THE PSYCHOLOGY OF SELLING

Proven Techniques, Strategies And
Scripts To Close The Sale Every Time

LEONARD MOORE

LEONARD MOORE

Copyright © 2018 Leonard Moore - All rights reserved.

In no way is it legal to reproduce, duplicate, or transmit any part of this document in either electronic means or in printed format. recording of this publication is strictly prohibited and any storage of this document is not allowed unless with written permission from the publisher. all rights reserved. The information provided herein is stated to be truthful and consistent, in that any liability, in terms of inattention or otherwise, by any usage or abuse of any policies, processes, or directions contained within is the solitary and utter responsibility of the recipient reader. under no circumstances will any legal responsibility or blame be held against the publisher for any reparation, damages, or monetary loss due to the information herein, either directly or indirectly. Respective authors own all copyrights not held by the publisher. The information herein is offered for informational purposes solely, and is universal as so. the presentation of the information is without contract or any type of guarantee assurance. The trademarks that are used are without any consent, and the publication of the trademark is without permission or backing by the trademark owner. all trademarks and brands within this book are for clarifying purposes only and are the owned by the owners themselves, not affiliated with this document. The author wishes to thank 123RF / gajus for the image on the cover.

# THE PSYCHOLOGY OF SELLING

# TABLE OF CONTENTS

Free Bonus: 3 Insanely Effective Words To Hypnotize Anyone In A Conversation..................................................................................7

Introduction....................................................................................9

Chapter 1: What Makes You A Wow Salesperson?.....................12

Chapter 2: The Psychology Behind Buying Decisions................21

Chapter 3: Prospecting And Getting Appointments..................32

Chapter 4: Overcoming Objections And Closing Sales..............41

Chapter 5: Sales Techniques That Work......................................51

Bonus Chapter: Sample Sales Scripts..........................................58

Conclusion.....................................................................................65

Other Books By Leonard Moore...................................................66

# THE PSYCHOLOGY OF SELLING

LEONARD MOORE

## FREE BONUS
## 3 INSANELY EFFECTIVE WORDS TO HYPNOTIZE ANYONE IN A CONVERSATION

If you're trying to persuade and convince other people then words are the most important tool you absolutely have to master.

As humans we interact with words, we shape the way we think through words, we express ourselves through words. Words evoke feelings and have the ability to talk to the listener's subconscious.

In this free guide you'll discover 3 insanely effective words that you can easily use to start hypnotizing anyone in a conversation.

Go to **www.eepurl.com/cRTY5X** to download the free guide

LEONARD MOORE

# INTRODUCTION

Even though you don't realize it, we are all salespeople. We are either selling our best qualities to a new date or selling our expertise/experience to a prospective employer or selling our ideas to people or convincing our friend to join us for a weekend movie. Knowingly or unknowingly, we are all selling.

Whether you want to advance your social skills or get hot men/women or even pitch your startup idea to a funding company, smart sales strategies will give you an edge. Contrary to popular perception, sales is not just about figures. It runs deeper with psychology, understanding consumer mindset, and persuasion techniques.

In the end, it may boil down to revenue, but smart psychological techniques will help you reach your target and kill competition. Sales may be about math, but selling is an art. The good news is, anyone can master this art. It isn't a secret superpower that some people are just born with. It is a carefully cultivated and practiced skill that helps you ace just about any situation in life.

Also, from a commercial point of view, any business needs revenue to grow. It helps cover the company's operational overhead and determine steady growth.

There's no business without money, honey! It is the oxygen that keeps your business breathing. However vital it is to the existence of a business, you are seldom taught to sell. Somehow, selling is not perceived as a very positive knack. In colleges, people don't bother about training or learning how to sell.

Our social conditioning is what has led to the creation of this perception. Television media and film have often portrayed salespeople as hungry wolves waiting for their prey. These are the sleazy, deceptive and unethical people who are out to get your money by sweet talking or selling your plain lies. I don't blame you for thinking this way. Many of us view salespersons as liars whose only aim is to sell to you.

What reinforces this view is the fact that thousands of people take up sales as their profession without being sufficiently trained for it. They are not trained in the fundamentals of psychology, persuasion, overcoming objections and effectively closing the sale. They operate with a belief that all they've got to do is list the features of a product, and get the customer to buy it. This naturally leads to a negative customer experience. I mean, would you buy from a person who, in a staccato-like tone, says "da da da da da these are the features of the product. Now come on, buy it." Likely not.

The techniques you will learn in this book can be applied in almost any situation where persuasion is involved. You can pick up these smart strategies and put them to use right away to get results in not just your sales targets but also other areas of life. In fact, I'd say sales training is excellent training for social or public life. You meet new people every day, learn to handle objections, gain greater knowledge about the buyer's needs/psychology, look for a common ground, and handle rejection.

Rather than holding a negative view of salespersons as manipulators, view them as graceful persuaders who get people in win-win situations.

There has been renewed interest in the field of persuasion and consumer psychology. A new wave of salespersons who use solid psychological principles, attract the buyer's attention, arouse their interest and tap into their subconscious mind to create the right feelings related to the product or service they are selling have now taken over. They understand that at the root, it is about solving a problem or creating the desired feeling in the customer.

In its broadest sense, selling is all about understanding what exactly the customer wants and fulfilling that need. If you are still selling using traditional sales techniques, you are in for trouble.

It is time to up your game and reinvent the way you sell because now it isn't just about selling; it is about helping the customer buy!

# CHAPTER 1
## WHAT MAKES YOU A WOW SALESPERSON?

Ever wondered why while some people break one sales record after another, others barely manage to scrape through their targets. It is all about the approach and technique. How do you come across to your prospects? What is your body language while selling? How do you make yourself come across as more positively persuasive? How do you demonstrate a more resolute and less desperate personality? What are the qualities that a wow salesperson should possess?

Every salesperson operates with a different approach, attitude, and mindset. Fortunately, sales is a skill that can be learned not a talent that a person is born with. Anyone reading this can be a superstar salesperson by sharpening their persuasion techniques and understanding human psychology. These skills are broader and can be applied in any sphere of life.

Here's everything you've wanted to know about the attributes that can make you a superstar salesperson.

**Self-Confidence**

Self-confidence is the top skill for any aspiring salesperson to cultivate. If you simply do not have the confidence to go beyond the first sign of resistance displayed by the potential customer, you won't be able to sell. All our skills you pick up will be pointless if there is no confidence while selling.

If a potential customer doesn't appear interested in your product or service and raises objections, avoid taking it personally. You need to hold their hand and help them buy rather than sell. You've got to be confident and self-assured enough to control the communication and lead it in the desired direction. If you potential buyer sniffs self-doubt during the interaction, you've ruined your chances.

People are rarely inspired by those who come across as insecure or full of self-doubt. If you don't believe in your offer or yourself, how do you expect to convince others about it?

Keep your body language assertive yet friendly. Stand or sit in an upright position. Lean slightly forward to demonstrate interest. Slouching, tapping your feet and fidgeting with fingers (or an object) can be seen as signs of nervous, boredom or lack of confidence, which will discourage people to buy from you.

Never keep your arms or legs crossed. Leave them open to appear more engaging, friendly, flexible and relaxed. Crossings your arms and legs is a sign of mentally switching off or being closed to what the person is saying. It depicts rigidity or disinterest. The atmosphere will quickly turn hostile.

Shake hands with a firm grip to signify assertiveness, authoritativeness, and confidence. Nothing makes a more unflattering first impression than a limp handshake. It demonstrates a weak personality and makes you come across as nervous and filled with self-doubt. The correct way to do it is by holding a person's hand firmly and raising and lowering it two or three times.

Don't squash the person's hand completely or you'll come across as aggressive and dogmatic.

Also, avoid unblinking eye contact, or you'll come across as intimidating. Look away once a while to maintain a balance between looking suspicious by shifting your gaze constantly and appearing intimidating by keeping unwavering eye contact.

## The Ability to Influence

Can you inspire and influence people to take the desired action? Are you persuasive and convincing enough to lead people into immediate action? Understand that today selling is not about rattling off a list of features. That's passé! "Remember, features tell, benefits sell." Features are nothing but facts about your offer.

However, benefits have emotional underpinnings. Persuasiveness and influence are about being able to harness the power of benefits to get potential buyers to decide in your favor. When you communicate benefits, you appeal to their emotions and interests, thus making the offer appealing. Benefits tell your potential customer using the powerful WITFM principle – What's In It for Me? For example, "the store is open 24 hours a day" is a feature while "you can buy whenever you want at you own convenience" is a benefit. Benefits speak directly to the customer about how the offer helps them, whereas features talk about plain, cold facts about the offer.

A persuasive salesperson knows good selling is helping the customer buy by translating features into benefits. Because hey, at the end of the day everyone's looking for, "what's in it for me?" Leverage emotions by focusing on benefits. Mention how it will add value to their life. Make them feel great about the prospect of taking up your offer, and they are sold!

## Superior Listening Skills

Average listening skills will not help you become a superstar salesperson. I know a lot of salespeople who have the gift of the gab. They are impactful speakers but seldom care to listen. A great talker won't go too far without listening. Speaking the right things comes from listening and comprehending your potential customer's needs and aspirations.

When you listen, you ask the right questions and have a better idea of what exactly he or she wants. Also, it shows respect and considerateness, which gives you an edge over salespeople trying to push their offers down the customer's throat.

Asking the right open-ended question (super tip for knowing more about the customer) and then muting your inner urge to speak can help you listen to the customer's needs. Do whatever works for you to keep yourself quiet and listen. Resist the overpowering urge to interrupt with your two cents. Only when you force yourself to be quiet can you tune in to the voice of your prospect.

**Rapport Building**

I know luxury car salespersons who are trained to peep into the cars of their prospective customers to look for clues to strike a rapport-building conversation. For instance, if a salesperson sees a golf kit in the back of the car, they mention something about looking forward to a session of golf over the weekend or talk about how they try to get home early for a round with friends.

The psychology that we like and listen to people who we believe are pretty much like us. They seem "one among us," and hence the tendency to believe and buy into what they say becomes easier.

Building rapport and developing relationships help your prospects feel a sense of a belonging or affiliation with you, which helps establish trust. This leads to a beneficial relationship where they even become repeat buyers and evangelists for your offer. A strong network of satisfied buyers is the cornerstone of growing your sales figures.

**Self - Motivation**

Yes, you may have a boss from hell monitoring your

strategies or results. However, the will to grow, learn and invest in your skills should originate from within you. You are not a completed piece but a "work in progress." Though the basics of sales may stay the same, inner motivation will lead you to keep reinventing yourself by applying smarter tricks, techniques, and tools to grow your sales figures.

You need to keep innovating to stay on top of the game. For example, if social media is the next big thing on the promotion and selling scene, you've got to learn to keep up with fresher social media sales tactics. Keep expanding your innovation muscle by coming up with newer and more effective strategies to make your offer more irresistible for customers. Make it an offer they just can't afford to refuse!

Keep sharpening your skills, developing newer methods, and making your communication techniques even more effective. Keep up-to-date with information, not just your products and services but also those of competitors.

The drive to keep reinventing, innovating and improving should originate from within you. No amount of orders from your manager will make you do something unless your own goals deeply drive you.

While we are on the subject of how to be a superstar salesperson, let us look at a few golden rules of sales too

**Rule Number One: Help Your Prospects Buy**

Rather than pitching your product or offer down the customer's throat, help him buy. What's the difference between the two? Huge! Average salespersons sell, exceptional salespersons help their customers buy.

It is the difference between getting your prospect to buy anything that helps you complete a sale or meet your targets versus understanding exactly what they want and making the process easier for them by offering them something that will add a clear value to their life.

When you sell, you think about yourself. When you help the customer buy, you put him or her first. You demonstrate respect and concern for their needs and desires. There is a greater acknowledgment of what they are seeking and things are more considerate in helping them get what they want.

If you help your customers buy, you won't come across like a shark waiting to chew anyone who crosses their path with selfish and greedy motives. On the other hand, they'll see you as a buying guide or consultant who helps them buy what's best for them. See the difference in the overall approach?

Operate with a more respectful, thoughtful and helpful approach. Don't act contemptuous towards prospects and raise objections or seem disinterested in the offer. On the contrary, change your approach and listen to them to understand how you can bring about a positive shift in their perception.

For instance, if a prospect talks about how he/she doesn't want a credit card because it makes them spend more, talk about how they can, in fact, get access to interest-free money in advance if they start spending more wisely and clear their bills on time. Bring about a shift in their thinking to make a win-win situation. Break the stereotype of a slimy salesperson out to grab their money.

**Rule Number Two: Be Likeable and Affable**

Come on now even you wouldn't like a machine selling to you, however effectively it sells. Take any bunch of star sales performers and ask them what is the one factor that sets them apart from average salespersons and they'll likely say, "The buyers like us!"

Resistance on the buyer's part almost always originates from fear. Fear that they don't need the product, they are being fleeced, and that the salesperson is a sleazeball. If you are able to help them overcome these fears by establishing trust, they'll like you.

Your prospect has to like you before they like your product or service. They have to buy your personality and attitude first before they buy your offer. If they don't like or take to the person who is selling, they won't care much about your offer, irrespective of how amazing it is.

Conversely, if they feel comfortable and reassured in your presence, they are more likely to take action. Prospects are more inclined to buy from sellers who come across as trustworthy, friendly and considerate. When you demonstrate a respect for their wishes and show eagerness in understanding what they want by listening to them, there are high chances of taking the plunge.

Focus on building a solid rapport (even if you don't peep into their cars), smiling, listening to them and acknowledging, maintaining eye contact, being immaculately groomed and above all – making them feel that you are one among them. I know some of the best salespeople who share personal stories, opinions, and feelings to come across as more human and identifiable.

Another super tip that can be attributed to evolution is mirroring. It works at a subconscious level and dates back to primordial times. When you mirror or subtly imitate the body language, words, tone, gestures, and expressions of your prospect, you'll come across as more likable and relatable. They'll think you are similar to them, which will help establish trust. Gently mirror their actions and words without making it come across like you are mimicking them or making fun of them. For instance, if the prospect raises their glass to sip a drink, follow suit or if they are leaning against a table, subtly lean in the same position. Observe their words, moves, and expressions carefully to replicate them.

It makes them shed the mask of a clinical robot and come across as a likable, relatable person who is "just like us." The more potential buyers feel a sense of similarity and solidarity with you, the higher are your chances of getting them to perform the desired action. Focus on building that connection.

## Rule Number Three: Be Honest and Ethical

Break the notion that all salespeople are unethical tricksters by operating with honesty and integrity. Don't con your prospects into buying something they don't need or selling them low-quality products. There's no need to pitch unnecessary extras unless you want to jeopardize your long-term sales career for a few short-term benefits.

If you are pitching a good product or service, listening to the prospect's needs and being helpful, there is no need to lie. Being honest, ethical and trustworthy in sales goes a long way. Be straightforward and reasonable to create a positive impression. This will not just help your prospects take action now but also keep coming back for more in future.

By lying and being unethical, you may make that one sale. However, you'll cut the opportunity for all future sales. It gets even more unfortunate if they warn others against buying from you. Integrity helps in building your credibility as a salesperson and increases chances of repeat sales.

## Rule Number Four: Know Your Product Inside Out

If you don't know about the product, service or offer you are selling, you're in for big trouble. When you are unaware of the attributes of your product, there's no way you are going to find the right fit for your prospects.

Think of yourself as matchmaker whose job it is to find suitable dates for singles. The first thing you'll have to do to determine if two people are compatible enough to hang out together is to know their physical attributes, hobbies, personality traits, interests and more. If you don't know them well, there's no way you can find a suitable match. Similarly, if you do not know the attributes of your products or services, there is no way you will be able to find the perfect fit for your prospects. What a wasted opportunity!

You won't sound convincing or persuasive if you don't know a product or service well. There goes your chance to impress a prospect. Imagine looking dumbstruck if the prospect comes up with a technical query about the product/service? You lose the opportunity to come across as authoritative and experienced.

# CHAPTER 2
# THE PSYCHOLOGY BEHIND BUYING DECISIONS

Ever wondered what drives people to make the decisions they do? Understanding why people make the decisions they do will help you get them to make these decisions for taking the desired action. When you are armed with knowledge about what leads people to buy, your sales effectively increases.

Here are some psychological principles that people can use while making purchase related decisions.

## Emotions Drive People to Buy

Know why insurance companies can rake in millions in sales year after year? Simple, they cash in on one of our most basic emotions – fear! Similarly, cosmetic and beauty product companies are able to play on hope.

People buy to fulfill an emotion-based need. Human beings are wired to react impulsively and instinctively to emotions, which makes it one of the most powerful persuasion attributes.

Emotions are the hot buttons you press to awaken or stimulate the desired feelings in a prospect. Ask yourself before approaching a prospect, "What emotional hot button can I trigger here?" or "What are the feelings that will help him/her buy this?" Examine the why behind the prospect's actions.

## Facts Backing Emotions Makes it Irresistible

If you are playing on the emotion of fear by letting your prospect know that people who don't buy insurance suffer plenty of losses, back it up with clear facts and figures. Logic and emotion are one of the most lethal combinations in sales, which seldom goes wrong.

If you tell your prospect that their child will be left behind if he/she doesn't sign up for a lateral thinking learning program, back it up with figures. Those figures should include how it has increased the child's creativity, productivity, problem-solving mindset and intelligence of children who have signed up for it versus those who haven't. This is just an example.

Whenever you trigger a strong emotion, make it even stronger with supporting evidence. This helps prospects justify their emotions. It is like, "yes, I am right in feeling this way." For example, if a prospect is blown away by a car and wants to purchase it, he/she won't simply buy based on emotion. They will also look for technical specifications to understand if the car fits their needs. Of course, the car will make them feel great, but it should also help them justify the purchase rationally.

When people spend money on something, they don't like telling themselves they bought it because it fulfilled an emotional need. They need facts to justify purchase decisions. If you give them logical reasons to back emotional decisions, they will be sold.

## People Make Egocentric and Self-centered Decisions

If you want someone to take the desired the action, you've got to relate it to them personally. Unless a prospect is convinced that there's something in it for him/her, they won't buy. People are selfish. They won't buy because you have to complete your sales targets, or because you will get the commission. They will buy when they realize what is in the deal for them.

Help them understand what is in it for them by focusing on the benefits they will enjoy through your offer. Talk to them about how your product or service will add value to their life or make things easier for them. How can something increase the person's sense of self-worth? If a product or service boosts a prospect's feelings about his/her personal worth, it'll increase your chances of making a sale.

## People Look for a Clear Value

This isn't something you can precisely measure. It is an intangible attribute that prospects ascribe to a product or service. Value isn't as much about what you are selling or the actual price of a product or service as it is how desperately the buyer wants it or how he views your product/service versus others.

For example, people prefer certain brands over others because it offers them some intangible benefit. The association with a specific brand makes them feel good about themselves. It may help them feel richer, classier, smarter, more well-informed, etc. than others.

The product or service make save their time or money, or it can help them become more productive and efficient at work, or it can make them healthier. When an offer fulfills a clear need, there are greater chances of making a sale. Position your product as one that gives them a clear value, and they'll be happy to buy.

## How Psychology Can Help You Drive Better Sales

Salespersons who develop an understanding of human psychology accomplish greater results than those who rely purely on logic or technical knowledge. This is because they can leverage the most fundamental emotions of people on a subconscious level. Appealing to a person's logic is often not as effective as appealing to their impulses. It's like igniting a spark, which then grows into an overpowering or burning desire.

Logic per se is not a power-packed seller. It may help you make a few sales. However, the wow factor will be missing. The wow factor will come only if you can tap into the subconscious and fundamental psychological emotions of buyers to sell.

Using psychology for driving sales is a simple yet effective three-part technique

Create a need for a product or service within the prospect. "Like, hey you know what, people's life spans have reduced. There is a greater risk of dying from a number of ailments. What will happen to people you care about after you pass away? Of course, you need insurance."

There you have created a need by instilling fear and insecurity. Basically, you are creating a gap and then attempting to fill the gap.

Explain how your product or service satisfies that need

Look for a hidden hot button that tips the sale completely in your favor and turns the fence-sitter into a totally convinced buyer.

**Power-Packed Keys to Using Psychology for Driving More Sales**

*1. Don't Give Too Many Options*

Prospects slip into analysis paralysis if they are given too many options. The first psychological to make the process of decision making simpler for them is to keep your options limited. Of course, if you have a catalog of hundred products or services, you can't bring it down to three. Rather chunk products or services into categories and let them first pick which category is most suitable for them. Once they are clear about the category, let them select the appropriate item within their desired group.

This is exactly what retail giants and supermarkets do. They don't spread out a million products for the customer to pick from. Similarly, online sites make it easier for the customer to buy by categorizing stuff by price, colors, types and more.

## 2. Fear of Losing Weighs Higher Than Gaining

This is the way people's psychology works. They are more concerned about preventing losses than earning gains. So while logically even if it's the same, they'll fight hard to save ten dollars than gain ten dollars because man is more emotional than a logical creature. What is ours is often more valuable than what is not.

Prospects respond more positively when you tell them what they will lose or miss out rather than what they stand to gain through your offer. The fear of loss impacts more than the prospect of gains. For optimal impact, reiterate on what they stand to lose by not taking your offer.

## 3. Play on the Social Aspect

I have a friend who uses the power of social influence brilliantly to cut rocking sales figures. We all know humans are social begins who follow others so they can emulate what they are benefitting from. The guy I am referring to keeps telling his prospects about how other customers have benefitted from a certain feature or service. Sharing positive feedback with other people makes your pitch even more powerful. Begin with something like, "Here's something our customers have said or felt about xyz product or service." Give social proof wherever possible to build greater credibility.

It acts as the perfect reassurance or validation to make your prospects believe they are on the verge of making the right decision.

## 4. Fewer Stats More Stories

Use the power of anecdotes to sell your offer. Since emotions work more compellingly than logic for driving sales, anecdotes are more effective than plain stats when it comes to persuading prospects. Rather than rattling off numbers, tell them the story of how your offer added value to a client's life, benefitted them or made things easier for them. Stories are powerful sales tools, yet very few people are able to leverage them for increasing their sales figures.

## 5. Make it Scarce or Limited Time

You have a higher chance of increasing your sales figures if you create a sense of urgency by pitching something as scarce or limited period. When something is rare or exclusive or available in limited numbers, people don't want to be left out. They want to be the ones who grab their share of the pie before it gets over. Again, this is a primordial human tendency that sales professionals can cash in on.

## 6. Power of Reciprocation

Our society thrives on collaboration and cooperation ever since primitive times. When you go out of the way and do something for people, they instinctively feel the need to return your favor, even if they don't say it. They are subconsciously indebted to you. Get your prospects to feel that you are doing something that is beyond the daily job you are being paid for. Use a phrase such as, "Just so you know Tim, I am going to have a word with my manager to get this done for you."

Just present something as a favor that you are doing over and above your job, and they'll feel obliged to return the favor. Making your prospect feel indebted is a good way to get them to act.

## 7. Principle of Contrast

Think about it this carefully to understand how it works

on a subconscious level. If I tell you a wallet costs $300, you'll think it is expensive. However, if I tell you that the wallet costs $1300, but I am giving it to you for $350, you'll jump with joy. The idea that you bagged an exceptionally good deal may make you pay more for the product or service than if I had just originally quoted $300.

You'll go beyond your budget owing to the notion that you are saving or getting a superb deal. In fact, research has proven that this strategy not just makes prospects feel delighted with their purchases but is also likely to make them into repeat purchasers. Inflating the initiating price and then settling for a lesser one is a powerful negotiation tactic that can be used for increasing your sales.

*8. Evaluate Your Pitch from The Customer's Point Of View*

What you say is not as important as what your prospect hears. How does your pitch or presentation sound to the customer? Place yourself in your customer's shoes try to analyze how what you say sounds to them.

For example, let us say you want to leave a voicemail on the phone of a prospect, leave it in your box first to hear how you sound. You will be surprised. Would you respond to this message if you were the prospect? Chances are that you would not. Send your prospecting emails to yourself, and gauge if you are excited enough to know more about the product after reading them.

Keep hearing your words, positioning and pitch as a prospect. Understand how you would feel if a salesperson spoke to you in a similar manner. Would you be excited, curious and interested? No? Then why should your prospect be?

Make a pitch that you'd definitely respond to if you were the prospect.

## 9. Understand the type of buyer

- Neuroeconomic (yes there is such a field) professionals have identified three main types of buyers – Spendthrifts, Average spenders, and tightwads.

- Smart salespersons attempt to understand the type of buyer they are dealing with to customize their selling strategy.

- Tightwads are predictably the toughest to sell to since they don't part with their money easily.

If you are selling to tight wards, bundle products or services together to give them higher value or to pack in more for less. Throw in freebies, bonuses, discount coupons and free warranties. Reframe the value of your product or service and reduce tiny fees associated with it.

## 10. Highlight shortcomings too

Fiona Lee, a social psychologist, conducted research that concluded that buyers were more trustful of brands/organizations that admitted to their 'strategic failings' in comparison to those that blamed external circumstances for their problems (even if this was actually true).

The conclusion was that buyers are alight with organizations admitting to their shortcomings since it reveals that they are looking to fix the issue rather than letting flinging the responsibility on an external source.

Similarly, aren't we all likelier to trust reviews that are more balanced over reviews that simply gush about the product? It doesn't seem authentic or genuine if a salesperson only talks about the strengths of a product. However, if the salesperson speaks about the pros and cons of the product/offer in a more informed manner, the entire thing sounds honest.

The prospect is not misled into believing incorrect information about the product or offer, which increases the trust factor and overall customer experience. And we know the power of happy evangelists for your product/services, right?

When you mention shortcomings, you need to ensure they are attributes that aren't very vital to the customer and yet make you come across as genuine. It is similar to be being asked to mention your strengths and weaknesses at a job interview. You don't mention a weakness that is integral to the role. For instance, if being a team player is vital to the role, you don't mention an inability to work in a team as a shortcoming.

Similarly, if you are using this strategy for establishing greater trust with the customer, don't mention a shortcoming that is important from the customer's perspective. For example, if saving is vital for him/her, don't say, "This play may not help you save big, but it has plenty of other benefits." Mention other non-important shortcomings that are not likely to impact the prospect's decision yet make you come across as authentic.

## 11. Use inoculation effect

When you are aware that a prospect is caught between you and a competitor, sharing information about the competitor's sales strategy will make the prospect wary of being manipulated or persuaded. This way you are reducing the impact of those supposedly clever sales tactics on your prospects. The trick here is to keep things truthful and not indulge in exaggerated claims. Don't make up stories to show your competitor's in an unflattering light. If your lie is called out, you will be the unethical and dishonest business. Stick to the truth.

For instance, let us say you work for a tour company and your prospect is comparing the prices of a tour you are offering with that of a competitor. They come with something like, "but their tour is much cheaper." You are aware of the competitor's sales tactic of locking the customer into a deal and subsequently upselling attractions and experiences for additional charges once the deal is sealed.

You can mention this to the customer saying, "Mr. ABC, while our competitors are offering you a lower price, it is their tactic to keep selling additional attractions, sightseeing options and experiences at additional rates once you are locked in with the low price. In complete contrast, with our company, you get a one cost package that covers everything without any additional charges or upsells. It covers everything, and you don't need to pay another extra cent for sightseeing, attractions, and experiences." This way you are alerting them to the competitor's tactics.

*12. Introduce surprise elements*

Keep customers on their toes by introducing the surprise element. This doesn't necessarily mean dropping the price from $100 to $1. In a classic study helmed by psychologist Norbert Schwarz, it was discovered that even an amount as little as ten cents was enough to change the perception of participants who stumbled upon the money by surprise.

Throwing in a small additional value or reducing the price a bit can help introduce an element of pleasant surprise, which can tilt the scales in your favor.

If you want to play it cleverly to build a surprise element, don't mention any additional bonuses in the beginning. When you are sure the prospect is sufficiently convinced with only a little doubt against the taking action, go for the kill with bonuses. Your fence sitting customer (who is already partly convinced) will lap up the surprise element and immediately decide to take action. You've just made the process of decision making easier for them by adding a surprise element.

## 13. Fast Solutions

Multiple Magnetic Resonance Studies have revealed that the human brain's frontal cortex becomes extremely active when a person thinks about waiting to get something. This is something that is a downright no for sales. Instant gratification is the key when it comes to making sales.

Ever wondered why if you really want a dress which is available for half the price online, you still go and purchase it at a full price from a store near you? You don't want to wait until it arrives.

Similarly, fast solutions, quick fixes, instant service, fast shipping and similar things are more appealing for prospects. If a product or service gives them instant pleasure or solves a problem, it becomes a good incentive for them to take action. Now you know why Domino's Pizza is killing it with their 30 minutes or free delivery policy. Customers are looking for fast solutions and pleasures.

# CHAPTER 3
# PROSPECTING AND GETTING APPOINTMENTS

A majority of sales processes follow a similar pattern or comprise seven distinct stages. Most people who are struggling to up their sales figure stumble at one or more of these stages, while comfortably handling the others. For instance, you may be a great conversationalist and prospector. You don't have trouble prospecting people. However, overcoming objections may be challenging for you. Similarly, others have trouble closing sales though they are excellent at prospecting.

Here is how a typical sales cycle works and how you can play your cards effectively throughout the process to successfully close a sale.

**Prospecting**

Salespeople generally get a lead or a prospect list from their organization. Others use innovative methods for meeting prospective customers such as attending seminars, business conferences, networking events and chamber of commerce memberships. Parties and informal gatherings are also great places to identify your target audience. Weed out people who aren't a fit for your offer rather than blindly pitching to all and sundry.

Identify your target audience on the basis of their motives, desires, demographics, concerns and desperate problems. For instance, if you attend a network marketing presentation, you know the target audience is a group of people who are looking to supplement their income or make money in their free time. If you are planning to sell a money manifestation course, these may be your ideal buyers.

Learn to identify your prospects by aligning what you are selling with their deepest fears or aspirations.

Here are some sales prospecting master keys

-Build rapport by focusing on commonalities between you and the prospect

- Tell prospects why you are contacting or calling them

- Avoid hackneyed cheesy sales pitches and instead ask something like, "is this (challenge or opportunity) something you are keen on (experiencing or solving). If they reply in the affirmative, set an appointment by informing them that you'd like to discuss the strategies in detail face to face.

- Remember you are not selling at this stage. You are only pre-qualifying prospects to know who your buyers are.

- Don't give up on the first stance of objections such as budget, need or other concerns.

-Ask more open-ended questions to know more about the prospect's needs. You'll come across as more interested and concerned about their requirement rather than just starting with what you have to offer.

Sometimes when you cold call or prospect clients, they will ask you for more information in a bid to put you off. They have already made up their mind about your offer not being relevant to them. A seasoned salesperson won't give up.

-Rather than simply mailing them information, grab the opportunity to open them up to a conversation or build rapport. When you send the material, you'll leave the onus of a follow up on the prospect, and in all likelihood, they won't get back to you.

"I'd be glad to send the information to you Mr. Smith. We have a 200 product catalog that can be emailed to you. However, if you don't mind, I'd like to ask you a few quick questions to ensure I only send you stuff that is relevant to you?"

"Sure, I'll do that immediately. However, I want to ensure the product on offer is a great fit so let me ask you a few quick questions." This is where you can shoot your qualifying questions to determine if you should book an appointment with them to take it further.

-One of the most powerful ways to build a prospect list is to ask happy clients for referrals. They'll spread a good word about your offer and give you access to even more prospects to build a close-knit community of happy buyers.

According to a 2003 published Harvard Business review piece, the value of a customer does not lie only in what he or she purchases. How your clients feel about your business/brand and how they speak about it to others greatly influences your overall revenue and profit.

The ideal time to ask for referrals is right after a completed sale. The reason behind this is, the sale has evoked fresh feelings of excitement and enthusiasm in him/her. The positive experience and excitement will translate into the new buyers wanting to share their happiness within their social circle, which will increase your chances of getting referrals.

-This is a small tip that I have seen many salespersons use to boost their sales strategy. They make every effort to keep in touch with existing customers, often arranging a meeting with them just to say "hi" or "catch up over coffee" or to know "if everything is fine with the product or service." They'll send birthday cards and extend invitations to exclusive customer events. How about sharing white papers or other content that you think will be valuable for your customer? No one thinks much about this strategy but staying in touch with existing customers can help you win plenty of referrals.

-If you are doing a cold call, disarm the customer if you want to get them interested and curious. A majority of customers will be busy when you call. If you simply start your sales pitch with who you are and what you are selling, there's little chance of you breaking the ice with them. There's a natural switch off button that triggers in their mind when it comes to sales.

The trick is to say something alarming that grabs their attention. "Hi, this Ashley Rogers from XYZ company. And I bet I caught you in between something important." They'll be like "huh." Get them to lower their guard and be less suspicious of pesky salespersons.

Mention the purpose of your call clearly with something like, "the objective of this call is to get 5-10 minutes of your time to discuss how you can reduce your documentation time by half and save 30 percent while doing it?" There, you've hit your prospect straightaway with the value proposition.

Always end with a question about whether the prospect is indeed serious about getting the desired results. Make them feel that if they are serious about making their life easier or saving money or whatever else they are looking to accomplish (or solving a problem).

-Always take the time to pick the right fish from the ocean by categorizing people into demographics, interests, hobbies, industries and more. You can't take on the entire ocean in one shot.

Begin by creating the ideal customer profile. Who is your ideal customer? For example, if you are selling a fairly expensive GPRS chip to parents of school students that helps them keep track of your child's moves, who is going to be your ideal customer? Probably, well-educated and professionally well-placed young families who are concerned about their child's safety and can afford to invest in the chip.

Do research to determine who your most profitable customers will be based on studying buying trends of similar products. Again, who are your worst prospective customers or clients who aren't likely to buy? Create multiple customer profiles, and the match them with existing prospects to find your best buyers. This way you'll focus your efforts on the best fish rather than trying to catch them all ineffectually.

- Humor is one of the best ways to break the ice and get people interested in your business. Who doesn't love laughing? Who doesn't fancy lightening up a bit now and then? People visualize salespersons as robots who clinically rattle off information about their products and services. This means you disarm your prospects when you use humor and come across as a fun person, not the sales individual they imagined.

Using humor to sell services several purposes. It makes people feel comfortable. For example, when you use self-deprecating humor, it instantly warms the prospect to you revealing your funny side and confidence in yourself. It makes you come across as human. Humor also makes you come across as a more confident and self-assured individual who is able to laugh at himself/herself or take things in a lighter spirit.

Also, humor makes your pitch unique and memorable. If a prospect has been through several uninspiring pitches for the same product or service, he/she is like to remember your humor based pitch. Insert humor, jokes, lighter incidents and anecdotes into your pitch to shake them up from their boredom and get them to feel more excited about your offer. It is like shaking them up and grabbing their attention.

## Set Up an Appointment

This can be a tricky one. Most people will come across as extremely positive about your offer face to face and promise to follow up with you but, they'll hesitate when it comes to setting up an appointment unless you've really managed to grab their interest (in which case they'll be calling and chasing you).

If a person mentions that someone else will be a decision maker along with them, at the onset insist that you conduct a joint presentation for all decision makers rather than addressing each one separately.

Use the "get your foot in the door technique" to bag appointments with prospects. The technique originated from door to door salespersons that put their foot in people's doors to prevent them from banging the door on them. This gave them a few more precious minutes with the prospects.

In the modern era, the foot in the door can be used by creating trust (build rapport when you approach them, do a non-salesy casual introduction, keep in short and simple), qualifying prospects (by posing the right open-ended, problem revealing queries) and positioning value or a solution to those problems.

Request a time of the prospect's choice since you don't want to catch them when they are constantly interrupted. This way you won't come across as a pushy intruder. However, at the same time, ensure that it isn't further than the next 3-4 days or your prospect will lose interest.

Do not start selling. Your job at this stage is to simply set an appointment by getting your foot in the door. If you start selling straight away, you'll lose that opportunity. Salespersons are hardwired to sell, unfortunately. Intrigue a prospect enough to actually make him/her look forward to the appointment.

Again, reveal a genuine desire to help. Don't pressurize

them into buying or listening to you. Rather, identify their most compelling problem and pitch your offer a direct solution to that problem. Offer them a value proposition that's hard to resist.

"Do you want to keep paying additional operational costs or do you want to save your operational costs by 30%. The decision, Mr. Smith, is yours." A statement like this will hit them hard, and there's little chance of them wanting to refuse something that helps the save. There again, how you posture or position your offer is all that matters.

Make saying yes easy for your prospect. Face to face meetings require a huge time commitment, and the prospect may not be ready for it. However, the prospect may be open to a phone presentation. Don't make it an all or nothing proposition if they refuse a face to face meeting. Go ahead and pitch the offer over the phone if you can by fixing a day and time for the call.

Another pitfall to avoid is delivering a rehearsed, word by word sales pitch that is a complete turn off for clients. A majority of them will never fix an appointment with you ever. Your script may be flawless, but you won't come across as a human. Plus, you'll never cover every possibility or type of prospect in a pre-written script. And sometimes, you'll have no choice but to go with a script. Think of multiple objections and scenarios a prospect can come up with at this stage.

The trouble with most salespersons is that they expect standard pre-determined responses from their prospects. Your prospect is not bound to go by your script. Listen to them keenly to understand their unique concerns and priorities, which you can build upon.

Again, your chances of setting an appointment will increase if you focus on the WIIFM principle. Tell your prospect what is in it for him/her. Make the call flow seamlessly and not forced.

Don't use words such as "interested," "buying," "selling" etc. There are certain words and phrases that immediately trigger a red flag in the prospect's mind, a post which they will switch off from everything you say. There's no point in asking a prospect if they are interested in something.

You've already determined that the product/service is relevant to them. If they say no, you'll have to comply or come up with a smart rebuttal and if they say, you'll be forced to go all salesy and list more information about your products or services. Focus on words such as "save," "value" "useful" etc. It should be pitched as something that serves their purpose and not helps you rake in a few quick bucks.

Another sales trigger is when a salesperson is overly formal. This will most likely cause your prospect to go away/hang up without scheduling an appointment. If you go, "Hello, my name is Jason Smith," the prospect will say a subconscious "bye" to you already. It is a definite robotic sales call alert. You won't sound authentic or trustworthy with anything you say after that.

Replace hello with a more casual and informal "hi" or "hey" It is alright to leave your guard down and appear friendlier. "Thank you" can be replaced with "thanks" and "have a good day" can be substituted with "goodbye." Come across as a person they can have an engaging conversation with.

If you are calling people in high positions or decision makers, call during "off hours" These well-insulated folks are not mentally equipped to take any more grind during their work hours. It is easy to switch off when you are in the middle of something important or mentally exhausted. Catch them when they are likely to be in a fresher mood, say early morning or late evenings. I don't mean to make you call them during dinner time.

Just call on the official number during non-peak hours. This also serves another purpose. It makes your prospect think you are dedicated enough to put in extended hours of work to serve the company and client, which reflects positively on your overall persona.

# CHAPTER 4
# OVERCOMING OBJECTIONS AND CLOSING SALES

Few things are more disillusioning for a salesperson than an objection that comes out of nowhere and hits you hard in the face. You are like, "oh! What do I say now, there goes my sale."

If you have had enough of "oh, you are too expensive," or "oh, this isn't my priority at this time" or "I don't have time for this." Or any other negative statements when it comes to closing the sale, it is time to pull up your socks and overcome these objections using smarter strategies.

Overcoming objections is the master key to being a successful salesperson.

**What exactly is a sales objection?**

A sales objection is a concern or reason cited by a prospective customer for bringing the sales process to an end. Sales objections often cover some hidden concerns that the salesperson should attempt to unmask for overcoming these concerns. By mastering these objection overcoming techniques, you won't squander good sales opportunities.

Here are common objections and how you should tackle them like a pro

## Objection One: "The offer/product/service is too expensive"

There is a price, and there is a value attached to everything. If you are looking at the price, you should also consider the value.

Make your prospect understand how the offer can help them save time or money, improve their lives, increase their effectiveness, etc.

"Don't you think this can help you save time?"

"Don't you think this can help you become even more productive?"

"Don't you think your family will be safer?"

Ask questions because in sales questions are often the answers you give your prospective customers. When you ask them, "don't you think it will help you save money?" you are telling them that their objection is unfounded and that this offer will help them save money.

Get them to reply in the affirmative to as many questions as you can in response to their objection. Research has proven that if you manage to get 'six yeses' in a row, they will be likelier to buy from you. You've brought about an affirmative shift in the mind by getting them to think positively about the offer.

In this instance, you have to demonstrate how the value or savings derived from the offer far exceed its cost or buying price. Once the prospective customer grasps the real value of what you are offering, it is easier for them to decide in your favor.

You can also try something like, "I agree this may cost more than what you expected. However, you don't want a cheap service that doesn't solve your problem or offer value. Cheap products or services are not effective for solving problems. The key is not the cost of a product but whether it solves your problem effectively. Imagine the cost of not being able to solve this problem with a cheaper product?

The high-cost objection can also be responded to with, "Let me share an instance or case study that will help demonstrate how the value of this product or service far exceeds its cost."

Now you've shifted the focus from high cost to higher value.

If you are prospecting via email, write a straightforward mail that strongly focuses value proposition. Use simple yet compelling language. This is the fastest way to reach a decision maker because it is tough to get people to put you through them on the phone. Instead, you could say. "We have something that can help you (value proposition). Who is the best person to talk to about this?" They will share email details more willingly.

**Objection Two: This isn't a priority at the moment**

This is another tricky objection that throws a lot of salespersons off the gear. However, there are smarter responses to every supposedly smart objection.

"I am slightly off the track. Can you help me understand what your priority is currently?"

Ask sufficient questions until you've established what is important to them at the moment. Once you successfully determine their priorities and challenges, weave your offer around these priorities.

For instance, if someone says investing in automated software is not a priority for their business, ask them what is important for their business currently. They may come up with "increasing profits, focusing on satisfaction and other similar replies."

"When you free up your time by investing in automated software, you have more time to focus on the product or service. This invariably leads to happy customers and boosts your customer satisfaction quotient."

"You'll spend more time on product development and diversify your portfolio rather than mundane administrative tasks, thus paving the way for more profits."

The idea is to closely connect the offer to what they mention as their priority.

"Our priority currently is keeping costs low, so we don't want to invest in this software."

"If keeping costs low is a high priority you'll cut down a lot of staff salary by investing in a more efficient and automated process." See what we did there? We took their objection and turned it on its head to help them understand that contrary to what they believe, it does indeed fit with their priorities.

At times, prospects will say something is not a high priority because they are masking another concern. To get to the bottom of that concern, you'll have to keep asking the right questions.

"If you have another concern Mr. ABC, I'd really appreciate you discussing them with me since we are always striving to enhance our services." You come across as a concerned representative of your business rather than a hungry shark looking over its prey.

Other times, they'll come up with something like, "I am too busy at the moment, call me in a couple of months." If they are claiming to be busy, they'll most likely give you the same reason after two months because the real reason is they don't think your offer is worth giving time to or considering.

Nix this notion by reiterating the value proposition of your offer. "Our offer can help you boost profits or save time within the next three months. And I can get you started on it in less than 30 minutes."

If they mention they don't have time to close the deal, talk about how the offer or product will, in fact, help them save time. When they say it isn't a priority or it isn't important enough to take up their time, make the offer a priority. Again, prioritize your solution as a fast and effective one that won't take much of their time and will, in fact, help them save time in future.

**Objection Three: "I don't want to change anything currently, I am happy with the way things are going"**

"Yes, I agree there is an element of risk involved in adopting new systems. However, with time you'll realize that there is even bigger risk involved in not embracing change and adapting to new ways of doing things. The biggest risk in life indeed is taking no risk at all and stagnating."

Many people are averse to risks or trying something different or innovative. Adopting a new solution and giving up a comfortable way of doing things can be challenging. However, the approach is to tell them how they will lose out if they do not adapt to the new solution.

Demonstrates case studies and examples of how people in the past have been skeptical of trying your offer, and how this change has benefited them.

You can go a step further and talk about path-breaking changes and trends that have taken over the world that were once viewed with skepticism. How dynamics keep changing and evolving, and how it is important to keep up with times. Explain how important it is to stay relevant in today's times, and how the bigger risk is losing this opportunity.

Shift feelings of fear and doubt related to purchasing the product to fear if they don't purchase the product. Create a bigger fear of losing out. This can help them view the offer in a more objective manner rather than being intimidated by it. The bigger fear should be losing out on a great offer rather than fear of investing in a product that doesn't turn out to be great.

Human beings are often wired to experience a false notion of security. They won't change or unsettle things unless it becomes necessary. You'll need to create a sense of urgency and pitch something as necessary if you want to shift their perception.

**Objection Four: "Thank you for offering us this, but we already have someone we buy from"**

"I am not suggesting you change the current supplier or company. All I want is an opportunity to demonstrate how our brand, company or solution is different, and how we provide greater value to customers."

Your prospective client is operating an attitude that says, "If things aren't broken there's no need to fix them." The prospect obviously has no awareness of the differences between the current solution and the one you are offering since they haven't tried it.

Your strategy should be to fill this information gap equipped with knowledge about how your offer or product varies from what they are currently using to help them review their earlier hesitation. Have simple yet effective, easy to understand comparisons of how your solution scores over what they are currently using. Use a like for like chart/table to compare each attribute. They should be able to review the information easily and reconsider their initial opinion about your offer.

The positioning or angle makes all the difference in sales. If you position your offer as "replacing their present solution," they won't view it too positively. However, if you position it as something that "provides them an opportunity to consider a solution that can give them more value." Don't replace their current option; just give them an option to gain additional value. Bingo!

## Objection Five: "We Prefer an Established Brand"

"That is understandable. However, let me do a like for like attribute comparison to show you how we score vis-à-vis the established brand. If you are a new operator in the market, one of the biggest roadblocks is establishing an identity. Everyone is bound to be skeptical of new players. They choose to play safe by opting for known brands.

Small and mid-sized or new businesses should equip themselves to handle this objection. The most effective way obviously is to provide a like for like comparison.

When you are making a like for like comparison chart with an established business, keep attributes where you score over the business at the top. Once prospects realize that you score over the first few (or in their view the most important) attributes, they will be likelier to overlook the ones that follow it. If there's a third party comparison of your solution versus an established solution, use it to drive home your point.

You can also offer the case study of an existing customer who switched from the established business to your business, and how this smart decision has changed things for them. For them, there is a risk involved in trying a new player. You can minimize this risk factor by offering a free trial to help them see for themselves how your offer or solution can impact their lives. Complimentary trials or a 30/60 day money back guarantee may work well in de-risking the process of picking your offer over an established brand.

## Objection Six: "We don't have a budget for this"

"Well, I don't expect you to purchase anything right away. All I want to do is give you the opportunity to know what we have created and to help you decide if it is valuable to you."

Shift the focus from you or your product to the prospect.

This is one of the biggest and most well-kept secrets of sales. Put your prospect's need for the limelight, not your solution.

Understanding how the process of budgeting works for your prospect. Do they have a budget in place for what you are offering, which they've already spent? If yes, when do they assign a new budget?

"I want you to see how this product/offer/solution can help you save. For all you know, it may actually cut down your budget and offer greater value."

**Objection Seven: "I need to consult my wife, manager, business partner before making a decision"**

This is often a positive objection which implies that the prospect indeed thinks your offer is good enough and wants to run it through another person whose decision he/she trusts. However, it can also be an excuse to avoid closing the sale.

See this as an opportunity to get a breakthrough about who the real decision maker is. Don't be disillusioned when they request to consult someone else. Proactively offer to talk to the person about your product or offer by requesting a joint appointment at the earliest. "It is wonderful that you want to consult a person you trust before making this decision. Let me make the process easier for you two by holding a joint meeting."

At the meeting, focus on the decision maker rather than the original prospect because the latter is most likely sold and is only looking for a second opinion.

**Objection Eight: "I can purchase this for cheaper elsewhere."**

You are in a situation where the prospect is attempting to play you up against a competitor for negotiating a better deal. In all probability, they plan to buy the product or offer from somewhere else at a lower price.

The only way to beat the competition if you don't want to reduce your price anymore is to demonstrate how though the competitor is offering a lower price; you've packed in more value. You can throw in a free warranty, extended service contract or other bonuses that translate into higher overall value even though your price is higher. Think about this, if company "A" if offering you a product for $50, while company "B" is offering the same product for $65 with a six month free service contract, a few bonuses and a free upgrade, wouldn't you rather opt for "B" since it offers higher value?"

The golden rule is – when you can't beat a competitor in price, up the value of your proposition to pitch it as a higher cost but also much higher value than the competitor.

**Objection Nine: "I am not interested"**

People generally use this objection when they respond to a sales pitch on an impulse. This is the reaction of prospects when they think their time is being wasted.

Rather than contradicting the prospect, empathize with him/her. Tell him/her you truly know how they feel about salespersons pitching worthless products to them. Follow this up by informing them about someone who felt the same but actually benefitted from the offer.

"That's fine Mr. Smith, I understand exactly why you feel this isn't of interest to you. ABC client said the same thing when I first approached them. However, now they are using our product to help their children read and learn better. I understand how important it is for you to improve your child's learning and development all the time. Can you tell me why you'd not be interested in knowing about something that can positively impact your child's learning abilities?"

There, now you've got them thinking if they are serious about their child's development, they should consider what we are offering.

## Use Objections as Opportunities

Keep your main sales objection as a lever to knock the sale in your favor towards the end. Closing on an objection is one of the most powerful strategies to close a sale. Rather than viewing objections as challenges or roadblocks, use them as opportunities to close a sell with greater impact.

Let us show you an example:

Prospect: I need the cost for this to be under $1000.

Salesperson: Why is it important to you that the cost remains $1000?

Prospect: It is important for me that cost per product should be below $1000 because otherwise, we will be overshooting our budget?

Salesperson: "Okay, assuming that we can give you the product for under $1000. I can't promise you anything. Let us just assume for now that you can buy the product for $1000 per piece, is there anything else that will stop you from buying the product?" Or you will definitely move ahead with the sale if you get it at this price?"

You are actually qualifying whether the customer is genuinely concerned about the high price or they are simply offering an excuse to avoid closing the sale. There is also an attempt to uncover other objections they may come up with. You are basically fleshing out.

Contrary to popular perception negative customers are not the toughest to sell to. The fact that they are negative about some ideas can be used in your favor. If you can manage to change the negative to positive psychology, you've won it.

It is the apathetic customer who is toughest to please. They don't have any objection and don't care, which means you can't use any objection to create a strong emotion for closing the deal.

# CHAPTER 5
## SALES TECHNIQUES THAT WORK

Of course, every sales professional can do wonders with the right sales technique ammunition. However, traditional sales wisdom doesn't make sense anymore since times have changed and these strategies have become redundant. Here are the top sales strategies that work and ones you need to throw out of the window right away.

**Make the customer your hero**

Much like every story, your sales story has to have a hero. Who will it be? Easy, the customer! Don't make your company, product or solution the focus of this story. Play the role of a guide or mentor. You are present only to facilitate the change in their life, and help them adapt to a better solution.

Everything should revolve around the customer's challenges, untapped potential, benefits, and life. Center your pitch on how wonderful your product or service is, and the customer will go running in another direction. Talk about how wonderful your product or service is for him/her, and they'll be likelier to listen.

**Present contrasts**

Create a powerful value perception by narrating stories

with contrast. When you narrate customer stories, do not be shy to mention the before and after stages of customers using your products or solutions. Talk about how people were impacted by the product or how things changed for them. Talk about how their life became easier, more effective, more enjoyable, and less stressful or other similar positives after using your product. Contrasting personal stories are very powerful when it comes to making sales.

Ever wondered why review sites where product reviews are mechanically mentioned get far lower affiliate sales than sites that have people chronicling their personal experience or stories with products. Narrate stories with contrast. Don't be shy about connecting emotions and researched data.

The best way to persuade a customer is to talk about people who experienced a change in their challenging environment or life. The offer should be presented as a solution to something they are grabbling with or something that adds value to their life.

Even if it is a simple dress you are selling, focus on how a well-fitted garment will add to their confidence, make them feel great about themselves, help boost their self-esteem, make them look gorgeous, make them more impactful and effective at social gatherings or corporate meetings. Even a small product or services can be played up to be a life-transforming solution for your prospective customer.

**The buddy trick**

The buddy approach works well for salespersons that are amiable, warm and congenial by nature. This technique is obviously based on being liked by your prospect. Show interest in the prospective customer and try to establish an emotional connect.

Essentially, you are not a salesperson but a friend who is trying to help the prospect find genuine solutions to their problems or a real way to enhance some aspect of their life. You must come across as real and genuine otherwise it'll backfire, and you'll be one among several glib talking, manipulative salespersons. Fake concern can be easily spotted.

## Guru approach

This technique is appropriate for salespersons who are more focused on logic and facts while selling and aren't keen on emotion-based sales. If you are more practical than warm and amiable, emotional connections won't sync well. This approach is also ideal if you are dealing with intellectuals in high positions of authority, who are not easily moved by emotions.

Use facts and logic to drive your argument. You position yourself as the ultimate authority or expert in the field and rattle off numbers on fingertips. You are a thought leader, a solution provider, subject matter expert and experienced guide, who possess high knowledge-based credibility.

This approach needs plenty of work. As a salesperson, you have to keep working on learning relevant information and stay up to date with new industry trends/changes. Have independent views about dynamics within the industry and keep chronicling your knowledge on a blog. This way you'll come across as an influencer, which can help you drive more sales in the long run.

## Customer personality technique

This is about analyzing the prospective customer's personality type and then adopting a sales technique that suits his/her persona. You may have to use a single approach or combine multiple approaches to help the prospect buy. I know a lot of successful salespersons who analyze the personality of their prospects before customizing their pitch to get desired results. For example, a friendly, warm person may find decision-making challenges. He/she may need more reassurance and persuasion when it comes to taking action.

Similarly, if a person is suspicious or wary of smooth talking salespersons may need more evidence of authority and credibility. You need to focus more on building trust with a person who is always suspicious of people's motives. Similarly, a person who lacks confidence and doesn't trust his/her ability to make the right decision needs to be reassured by focusing on the value they gain from the offer.

**Product-oriented approach**

Here the hero of your story isn't your company or the prospect but the product you are selling. In the product-oriented approach, the salesperson is focused on listing the features, benefits, and specifications of a product.

It includes investing a considerable amount of time towards explaining the features and benefits of a product or giving product demonstrations/presentations until the prospect is persuaded about the true value of it. If you are using a product-oriented approach, you must know the product inside out, with all its technical specifications.

Preempt several questions regarding the product so you can answer them when they arise knowledgeably and authoritatively. Prospects are likely to come up with plenty of questions regarding the salient features and benefits of a product if you are using the product approach.

**Need-based selling**

The hero of this story is basically the solution of a compelling customer need, which you are attempting to fill. Using this approach, you attempt to uncover a clear and compelling need that the customer is desperately looking to resolve.

For instance, he/she may be lonely and looking for a date or a relationship. As a dating site registration salesperson, you have to tap into that need and get them to sign up for a suitable membership plan. What you are doing is identifying a need and then pitching your offer as a solution for that need. You are posing as a problem solver, who can fulfill the customer's need.

Rather than creating a new need, you are filling an existing need.

**Soft Sell versus Hard Sell – What Is The Difference**

Soft selling is a technique that is much appreciated by prospects especially when they need gentle guidance and suggestions when it comes to making a purchasing decision. The seller uses subtle persuasion and suggestions to reassure or convince a buyer. This sales technique is more subtle and non-aggressive. For instance, the salesperson may gently try to sway your mind with "we sold hundreds of these pieces last week" or "the lady who walked in before you loved them so much she picked one in every color to gift her family."

You may have heard these gentle persuader's innumerable times. Soft selling can also involve recommending a specific product to meet your needs. "If you live in a warm region, this cooler with xyz benefits will best suit your purpose of keeping the house cooler during warm summer days." They may say, "I recently purchased the same product, and I am very happy with the results. It has helped me keep the house more temperature controlled while enjoying fresher and more purified breathing air." There's no pressure on the buyer to take action. He/she is presented with facts and reviews, based on which they can make a decision.

Hard selling, on the other hand, is a more aggressive and sales driven tactic that doesn't go down too well with buyers. In hard sell, prospects are sometimes intimidated or manipulated into buying stuff they may not even need. Hard sellers make a customer feel compelled or obliged to buy a product. They just won't take no for an answer. They create a need, a sense of urgency or a feeling about how the customer will lose out big time if he/she doesn't take action immediately.

Typical lines used by hard sellers are, "buy this today or miss out since we have a limited stock of these goods which will all be gone tomorrow." When a salesperson tries to decide on behalf of the customer rather than helping the customer make a decision, it is a hard sell technique. You are not giving the customer the time or freedom to make a decision. Rather, you are forcing your decision on him/her."

## Using reverse psychology for closing sales

As human beings, we are often resistant to persuasion. When you realize you are being convinced to do something the other person wants you to do so, you become psychologically resistant to the idea. We are not forewarned about how people try to persuade or manipulate us, which makes us develop greater resistance. So when the glib talking salesperson says, "you should really have this because it makes your life easier" the thought bubble over your head says, "There goes this moron trying to use his/her best persuasion tactics on me to get me to buy something I don't need."

As a salesperson, leverage reverse psychology to your advantage!

For instance, disqualify your potential client. This only works if you are being honest. Be mindful of the fact that it can also offend your prospect.

Let's say you go shopping for a baby cot and the salesperson seizes you up to gauge what kind of baby cot you are looking for and what is your budget. You find a one of its kind, a gorgeous baby cot that is supposedly handcrafted and made with the finest quality material. The salesperson says, "You won't be able to afford that, or that's not within your budget, I'll show you something more affordable." How will you feel?

Now, if you have even a shred of self-respect in you, you would want to prove that snooty salesperson wrong by demonstrating that you can, in fact, afford the baby cot, even it means you go without lunch for six months. When someone challenges your sense of self-worth, you feel a compelling urge to prove the person wrong. This feeling can be harnessed brilliantly by a smart salesperson. However, it is tricky and should be used with caution, only if you are sure it will pan out as intended, otherwise you'll end up offending the prospective customer for life.

Presenting something as off-limits for a prospect and showing them more affordable, budget-friendly options only triggers a strong willingness to stretch beyond their intended budget. Again, don't use this as an evil manipulation trick. View it is a persuasion technique that can be used if you genuinely believe that the high cost will also offer them high value or the product is really useful to other. However, you are just another evil shark out to grab their money.

# BONUS CHAPTER
## SAMPLE SALES SCRIPTS

**Cold Calling Sales Script with Objections**

Customer: Hello

Sales Agent: Hi there, Can I take just 2 minutes of your time and tell you how you've been paying way too much all this while for high-quality tires and other truck parts?

(No asking – Is this the right time to talk to you. Customer will most likely say no)

Customer: What??? Okay go on

SA: Perfect. Let me help you save right away.

Customer: So what is this about?

SA: We are a truck driver-focused company formed by truck drivers who know the real value of your time and money. We know about the hassles of being late and of being stranded on the road owing to defunct parts. This is why we are here to help you buy high-quality tires and other parts while saving a lot.

We are not just another big company out to get your money, but former truck drivers who want to help you save. We want you to know that we are here to give you the best without costing you a fortune.

Customer: I already have a supplier whom I buy from regularly?

SA: Very well. You sure must be happy with the existing supplier. But what's the harm in trying something that can probably give you a much better deal than what you are currently getting? What if we can help you save a lot while giving you great service. What do you have to lose by trying us? We are so sure you are going to love us.

Customer: I don't have time for it right now.

SA: I understand the importance of your time. That's why we are here to help you save both time and money.

You can order right away from the convenience of wherever you are, and we'll send it to your doorstep. It's that simple. No gimmicks. No catch. No waste of time.

With us, you will have the opportunity of using the best quality tires for a wide range of trucks at the lowest prices.

Customer: I need more information before ordering

SA: No problem. Take your time. Go through our catalog/website and see for yourself the quality and prices we offer our customers. However, I do not want you to miss out on a current offer we have going where you can get (mention any current running offer).

It's easy. I can give you all the information you are looking for, and you can order straight away. We have a special offer where you can buy XYZ for the best price right now over the phone.

I can send over a representative who can explain everything to you in detail at a time convenient to you. He will show you how you can save on purchasing high-quality truck parts at the best price. Wouldn't you like to know how save on truck parts you are already purchasing?

Customer: Do you have a money back guarantee?

SA: Yes we have a 30-day Money Back Guarantee to help you order with absolute peace of mind.

Customer: I am not looking to buy this particular part now.

SA: Yes I understand. You may already have one right now. But don't you think it's practical and hassle-free to keep a spare part handy rather than running around at the last minute when you will really need it. Plus you may end up paying much more at that time. Wouldn't you like to order at a lesser price today than spend more later?

And buying today can help you save $$$. We have a special offer only for now (mention offer). Don't you think you can save a lot by ordering during the special offer period a part of which you will end up paying much more later?

Ask close-ended questions where the customer has to answer yes.

If many yeses. You've gained an upper hand. The deal is yours.

Customer: I pay the same price when I buy this form XYZ, so I'll stick with them.

SA: what if we can match the price or give you a better price? Would you consider buying from us? Let's make the deal, even sweeter, for you. We will even throw in free shipping if your order goes above $50.

Customer – I am interested. How do I go about this?

SA – You can place an order with me right away and have the part delivered to your doorstep without any hassle. Alternatively, you can also log in to our website xyz.com and order online at the click of a button. It's that simple.

SA – Would you like me to guide you to ordering from the website right now?

Customer: Yes, please.

SA: Go about explaining how to order from the website.

Customer: You are a new company, I'd rather not order from you and stick to an old, reputed firm.

SA: As I said earlier, we are here to help you buy, and not just sell and we have been drivers ourselves, so we know the importance of getting you back home quickly by saving your time and money on the road. There's no harm in trying us. We might help you save a lot of money. Let us help you buy once, thank us later. You deserve the best price. Let us give you that.

Customer: Why Should I Order From You?

SA: We bring you the best quality tires and products at the most affordable prices. We actually have a huge variety of high-quality parts that you can order right from the comfort of your home. It's fast, easy, affordable and very convenient for you.

Customer: Where do you source your goods from?

SA: We source our goods from the best manufacturers all across the globe to bring you the best possible parts at the lowest possible price. We conduct thorough checks and quality standard ratings to ensure that you get nothing but the best. Our products are guaranteed to give you a hassle free time on the road at honest prices. Give us a try. You won't regret.

Customer: What items do you stock?

SA: We stock a huge variety of items that includes top quality commercial tires and rims, Volvo replacement parts, international replacement parts and Freightliner replacement parts. Whether you are looking for steer tires, drive tires or trailer tires, we've got it all covered.

We have it all available in stock, ready to ship right away. You just have to place your order with us today, and we'll have it zip across right away.

Customer: Can you give me a discount?

SA: Our prices are already the lowest you can find anywhere in the market. Since we ourselves have been drivers, we think about our customers, care for them and have hence kept the profit margins low. We always help you buy first rather than just sell you stuff.

## Cold Calling Sales Script for Setting an Appointment

Hi, this is Roger from Skyline Solutions.

We've been working on some rather path-breaking solutions that will help track your child's moves and ensure they are safe all the time. Isn't this something you'd like more information on?

Yes.

Great, so we've created this tiny chip that can be fixed anywhere from the identity card of the child to his/her bag for helping you monitor their moves. It is safe, radiation-free, easy to fix and use and best of all – cost-effective.

We've helped several parents in the city keep their little children safer by keeping a close watch on their moves.

Can I ask you a few questions? (Go with the six yeses theory described in objection handling)

Is your child's safety important to you?

Wouldn't you like to know more about your child's movements?

Wouldn't you like to be alerted if your child is in some danger?

Wouldn't you want to know if he/she is regularly attending classes?

Wouldn't you want to invest in something that can be life-saving for your precious little one?

Wouldn't you like to enjoy more peace of mind where your child is concerned?

There, you've not just asked qualifying questions to know if you are indeed speaking to the right person but also subconsciously imprinted into their mind how they just cannot do without this product.

Once the prospect replies in the affirmative to your queries, you jump at the opportunity to schedule an appointment.

Great! I think the best place to begin is by scheduling a meeting so I can help you understand how the product can be of immense value for your family. "Is Tuesday a good day to talk to you?"

If we want a clear response for day and time, don't throw it open like, "when is the best time to meet you?" If they are not too keen on fixing an appointment they'll say, "I'll let you know later."

Rather, come up with a clear date and time, "How does Tuesday 5 pm sound to you?" If they are busy, they are likelier to say, "No. I am a bit tied up on Tuesday. Let's meet on Wednesday during lunch at 1 pm." There by giving a clear date and time, you increase your chances of getting them to commit to a fixed date and time.

If they can't make it on the day and time suggested by you, they'll feel obliged to come up with a time of their choice, thus helping you lock them into an appointment. Again, this works at a psychological level when it comes to persuading a prospective buyer to agree to a meeting.

# CONCLUSION

Thank you for purchasing the book.

I genuinely hope it has offered you several proven sales strategies, tried and tested persuasion techniques and a treasure of practical psychological sales tips. These tips can actually be applied just about anywhere, in any situation from sales to interpersonal relationships to negotiations. It'll help you understand the sales process and learn some techniques along the way.

Whether you want to achieve record-breaking sales figures or simply understand how buyer psychology works to sell more effectively or learn brand new approaches to sale, this book is handy a resource.

The next step is to use the book and apply these proven sales strategies to achieve higher sales targets, better conversions and greater financial rewards.

Finally, if you enjoyed reading the book, please take the time to share your views by posting a review on Amazon. It would be much appreciated!

# OTHER BOOKS BY LEONARD MOORE

**Manipulation**
21 Proven Techniques To Secretly Manipulate, Persuade And Influence Anyone

Maybe you've been led to believe that brainwashing other people is something that can only happen in movies. Maybe you think that taking advantage of the subconscious mind is something only crazy people would try to do.

The truth is, as human beings we're imperfect. We have weaknesses. And if you study and get to know these weaknesses you'll have a huge power in your hands. When you master the right manipulation techniques, the real ones, it is completely possible to influence other people's thinkings and make them do what you desire.

In this book you'll find 21 of the best manipulation techniques, the ones that can easily give you access to almost anybody's mind. By learning and applying them, you will have the chance to create a great positive change in your life and reach your goals faster.

This handy manual will teach you:
- 21 Proven Techniques to Manipulate And Brainwash Anyone
- The Right Way To Disagree Without Sounding Disagreeable
- How To Interpret And Take Advantage Of Gestures
- Working Ways To Build a Relationship With Your Listener
- How To Mirror And Direct Others Without Anyone Noticing You
- Practical Strategies To Penetrate The Subconscious Using Keywords
- How To Set The Right Mood To Manipulate Others In A Conversation
- Common Mistakes And How To Avoid Them (The Majority of People Doesn't Know This)
- And much, much more

Learn how to get in control and live a life of happiness, success, joy, and peace.

**"Manipulation" is available at Amazon.**

## Hypnosis
21 Proven Techniques To Easily Hypnotize, Influence And Control Anyone

Imagine if you could direct other people's decisions. Imagine if you could influence people's subconscious minds and make them do what you want. Imagine if you could learn how to discover and take advantage of the hypnotic "reflexes" we all have.
Everything you're about to read is completely possible. Maybe you're not going to believe me. If this is the case, I feel sorry for you. So many people are already using hypnosis to direct other people's decisions and thinkings, maybe even yours.

The truth is, once you find a way to reach the subconscious you can easily direct the brain's decisions. As human beings we don't think like computers. Because of that we can be influenced easily. Hypnosis is just a way to take advantage of a pre-existing weakness.

I have already used three hypnotic practices to keep you reading, but you probably didn't notice. Imagine how powerful you can become by using the power of hypnosis and mind control in your own life.

Hypnosis is not some sort of magical fluff, it's a powerful, century-old psychological practice. Doctors and psychiatrists have been using hypnotic tactics to relax and anesthetize people, and the best salesmen take advantage of hypnosis every day.

You're about to learn 21 little known hypnotic techniques that could change your life. Don't worry, this book is not about magically creating "zombie people" that will follow every order. That is not hypnosis, it's fantasy. You're about to learn the real thing. The same methods world's most famous hypnotists use.

**Some hypnotic practices you'll learn to master:**
- Breathing Technique To Induce A Trance State
- 6 Little-Known Truths About Hypnosis
- How To Use Rapid Induction To Hypnotize Difficult Targets
- The 3 Phases Involved In Each Hypnosis Act
- How To Use Indirect Suggestions To Mislead The Conscious Mind
- The Hypnotic Bind Technique
- And much, much more

Don't let others control you. Buy this book today and start taking advantage of hypnosis in your life.

**"Hypnosis" is available at Amazon.**

## Mind Control
Forbidden Manipulation And Deception Techniques To Persuade And Brainwash Anyone

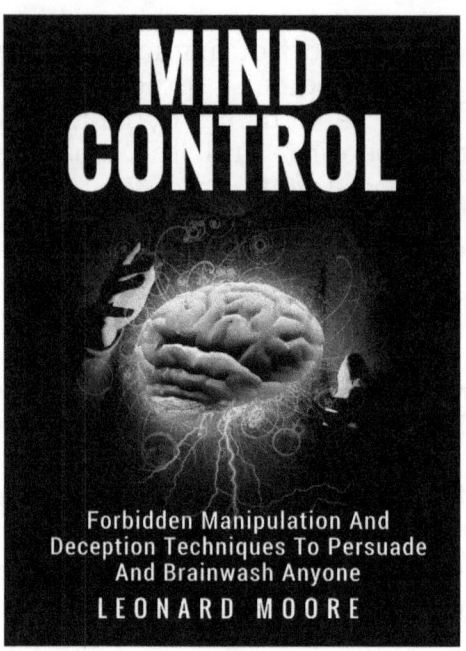

Mind control, also known as brainwashing, involves a unique selection of tools and techniques that will allow you to lead people in conversations and establish connections that have them genuinely wanting to do whatever you have asked them to do. In many instances, they will even do so thinking it was their idea to do so, and that you haven't planted the idea in their mind at all.

When you'll become truly skilled at mind control, you will be able to have and do anything you want. Whether you want to get a sale on something, make a sale, get money, go on a date, get a raise or a promotion, get more slack from your boss, grow your business, or do virtually anything else that requires other people to cooperate with your desires, you will be able to do so with everything you learn in this book. In addition to learning the important skills and techniques required to brainwash others, you will also learn how to never get caught.

You will learn everything you need to in order to be a master at mind control and genuinely create the life you desire without anyone ever knowing how you did it.
"*Mind control is a powerful skill you have to master if you don't want to be influenced and brainwashed*"
Remember, if this information is available to you, it is available to others as well! Knowing these techniques will prevent yourself from being brainwashed and will ensure that you are always doing exactly what you want to be doing, and that no one else is controlling your fate. This is all about putting you back in control of your own life.
In this book you'll also find real life examples that will teach you how to apply the techniques learned in the most effective and clever way to get results.

**You'll learn:**
- Proven Techniques of Persuasion, Manipulation and Deception
- How To Manipulate Others Without Never Getting Caught
- Working Strategies To Protect Yourself From Being Brainwashed
- All The Truth Behind Mind Control And Dark Psychology
- Mind Control Techniques Already Used in Society
- How To Stay In Control Of The Conversation
- Examples of Mind Control Techniques in Real Life
- And much, much more

If you want to change your life as you know it and start having the type of success that all of your idols rave about, then it is time to take back control. This book will give you every tool you need to do that. The only question is: are you ready for the life of your dreams?
Get the life you've always dreamed of!

**"Mind Control" is available at Amazon.**

**How To Analyze People**
21 Proven Techniques To Secretly Analyze People And Understand Body Language, Personality Types And Human Behavior

Imagine being able to secretly understand other people's thoughts and intentions. Think about the countless ways in which you could use this knowledge in your advantage. Imagine reading body language, word usage, facial expressions and subconscious actions to always know exactly how to behave in a business meeting, how to talk to that girl, how to successfully close a sale every single time.

Analyzing people is something we all do on some subconscious level. Whether you realize it or not, you're always profiling the people around you. Being able to take advantage of this skill and control it can be a powerful tool to use at your own leisure.

This book will teach you 21 of the best techniques you can use to secretly analyze people and learn more about them, the same techniques the most successful FBI agents use on a daily basis. Whether you simply want to understand people better, learn more about their motives, thoughts and feelings or develop deeper connections with others, this book will help you do just that. You'll also find real-life examples to better understand how successfully apply the techniques you'll learn.

**Some of the techniques you'll discover:**

- How To Effectively Read Body Language
- Core Principles Of Eye Reading
- How To Understand Someone's Values And Desires Through Actions And Cognitive Thoughts
- What The Way People Walk Reveals About Them
- How To Identify Different Personality Types
- How To Understand Someone Else's Thought Pattern
- 11 Of The Most Important Facial Expressions And How To Read Them
- How To Read A Person By Looking At His Or Her Environment
- A Simple Yet Effective Process To Re-brand Yourself To Be More Likeable
- How To Take Advantage Of The First Impression
- Tips And Tricks To Read People Using Their Handwriting
- How To Shape Someone's Perception With Your Body Language And Gestures

**Learn how to understand people's thoughts and perceptions and take control of the conversation.**

**"How To Analyze People" is available at Amazon.**

## How To Secretly Manipulate People
Discover How To Manipulate, Persuade And Influence Anyone, Taking Advantage Of Human Psychology

Do you want to get people to agree with you whenever you want? Would you like to know how influence other people's thinkings and make them do what you desire? Then mastering the art of manipulation is for you.

Manipulation is a practice whereby you look into someone's natural psychological tendencies and use them to help you get your way. You learn how to understand what people want and need, and what drives them to make decisions.

Then, you tailor your pitch or offer to get them to agree with you and give you what you want, while making it look like they were getting what they want! Ultimately, you lead the conversation by making it look like they are. In this book, you are going to learn exactly how to do this.

**In this manual you'll learn:**

- How To Analyze, Manipulate And Persuade People While Staying Secret About It All
- The 3 Most Important Steps Of Manipulation (Almost Everybody Gets These Wrong)
- How To Read Body Language, Facial Expressions, Verbal And Non-verbal Clues
- How To make others do What You Want By First Encouraging Them To Say No
- Practical Examples That Will Step-up Your Manipulation Skills
- Powerful ways Manipulate Others With Your Body Language
- A Step-by-step Solution To Recover Your Art If Somebody Discovers What You're Trying To Do
- How To Use Logic And Emotions To Control Other People's Thinking
- Secret Techniques To Protect Yourself From Getting Caught
- How To Overcome People's Trust Issues And Sneak Into The Subconscious

In a time where everyone is fighting to get to the top, you need a little more than great skills and a good personality to get there. Instead, you need to know how to successfully manipulate anyone so that you can "earn" your position at the top and keep it. If you are ready to start getting your way and experiencing far more joy and success in your life, this is the exact book for you.

**Take control of your life today**

**"How To Secretly Manipulate People" is available at Amazon.**

**Human Psychology**
21 Fundamental Principles of the Human Mind to Understand How People Think and Behave and Subconsciously Influence Their Actions

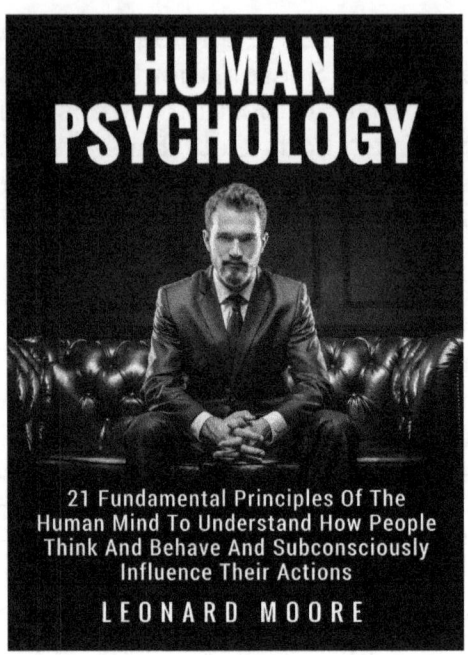

Human psychology itself is a vast topic that requires many years of research and attention to truly learn the entire subject. However, you likely don't have many years of time to invest in research if you want to start using human psychology to direct human actions and behaviors *now*. For that reason, in this book you'll find 21 of the most important human psychological traits that you should know if you want to use someone's psychology to influence and direct them to act and behave in certain ways.

Each of these topics will be explored in-depth, allowing you to understand what they are, how they work, why people experience them, and how you can use them to direct people's behaviors.

Whether you are a boss looking to have greater control over your employees or to create a more positive atmosphere, a friend looking to increase the positive energies and emotions experienced by your friend or family member, or someone who is looking to get people to do more for them effortlessly, understanding human psychology is essential. Not only will this help you understand behaviors themselves, but it will also help you understand what drives them and how you can use this knowledge to drive the behaviors yourself.

**Some precious lessons you'll learn:**

- How People Take Decisions And How To Influence Them
- How To Understand Other People's Perception And Take Advantage Of It
- Freud's Theory Of Personality
- Are Morals Always A Good Thing?
- Core Values That Drive Human Behavior
- How To Influence The Behavior Taking Advantage Of Emotions
- The Biggest Reason People Lie
- How To Get A Strong Willpower
- Psychology Behind Cheating
- How To Take Advantage Of Social Influence
- How Do Genes Influence Psychology?
- The Psychology Of Love And How To Take Advantage Of It
- And Much, Much More

**Learn the right principles to get in control!**

**"Human Psychology" is available at Amazon.**

**How To Hypnotize Anyone**
Discover The Secret Hypnotize Techniques And Language Patterns To Hypnotize And Persuade Anyone

If you have ever wondered about the mysteries of hypnosis, you are not alone. It's something that has always been surrounded by wonder and mystery. However hypnosis it's a natural phenomenon that people have harnessed and focused and if you learn the right techniques you too can successfully hypnotize other people and speak to their subconscious mind.

In this book you'll learn everything you need to know to hypnotize anyone using a step-by-step process, from induction to deep trance, to speaking to the subconscious as well as ending the session and setting up goals.

This guide will give you all the materials you need if you're starting from scratch, as well as more advanced scripts and hypnotic techniques to progress further. You'll get a strong understanding of the history of hypnosis, the different styles, philosophies, methods, and procedures that will open doors for you in your own practice. You'll also find answers to the most common questions like: How and why hypnosis works? What are we doing when we hypnotize people? What does it feel like? What are the conscious and subconscious? What is the difference between stage hypnosis and clinical hypnosis? Is hypnosis dangerous? Can I hypnotize myself?

**In This Book You'll Learn:**
- What Is Hypnosis And How It Works
- 3 Steps To Induce A Trance (With Exact Scripts You Can Use)
- Hypnotic Techniques World's Top Hypnotists Use
- Betty Erickson's 3-2-1 Script
- 5 Techniques To Focus Anyone's Attention And Sneak Into The Subconscious
- How To Hypnotize Anyone Using Breath, Voice, Memorization And Language
- The Staircase: How To Use Metaphors To Speak To The Subconscious
- Hypnotic Tips, Tricks And Secrets That Most People Don't Know
- How To Use Hypnosis To Help People Achieve Their Goals Easier
- A Complete Script To Take Someone From Beginning To End In A Hypnotic Session
- Myths And Frequently Asked Questions About Hypnosis

Believe me, once you get started with hypnosis you won't want to stop.

**Learn the real hypnotic techniques today!**

**"How To Hypnotize Anyone" by Leonard Moore is available at Amazon.**

www.ingramcontent.com/pod-product-compliance
Lightning Source LLC
Chambersburg PA
CBHW070209230526
45471CB00002B/895